Advance Praise for *The Book of Endings*

Leslie Harrison's truly marvelous new collection *The Book of Endings* works constantly at the edge of articulation, at the breakdown of language and thought: "what / remains is one person in a box is a system collapse / is sky holding ground holding stone holding hole / holding hands holding on black hole without end / the earth gave us everything took it back again." In these hauntingly incantatory lines, the Eucharist is elegiacally holding hands with the expanding and contracting universe, eternity with oblivion and recreation. Love, endurance, and the planet are all empty as a hole and yet, like these poems, solid as stone.
—Andrew Hudgins

The mother has died, the speaker's hair silvers in the moonlight, and spring, New Englandy as ever, does not come as promised. But "the sky keeps showing off   amusing itself" and the cold ground can be worked into "a blanket." Comfort is at hand in Leslie Harrison's *The Book of Endings,* poems of loss that yet offer uplift, music, words whose meaning, once unpacked, bring relief: "The final absence of air cyanosis," the speaker reminds us, is "from kyanous which is Greek which just means blue."
—Christine Schutt

Leslie Harrison

The Book
of Endings

Leslie Harrison
February 2017

The University of Akron Press
Akron, Ohio

Copyright © 2017 by The University of Akron Press
All rights reserved • First Edition 2017 • Manufactured in the United States of America.
All inquiries and permission requests should be addressed to the Publisher,
The University of Akron Press, Akron, Ohio 44325-1703.

21   20   19   18   17   5   4   3   2   1

ISBN: 978-1-629220-63-5 (paper)
ISBN: 978-1-629220-62-8 (cloth)
ISBN: 978-1-629220-64-2 (ePDF)
ISBN: 978-1-629220-65-9 (ePub)

LIBRARY OF CONGRESS CATALOGING-IN-PUBLICATION DATA
Names: Harrison, Leslie, 1962– author.
Title: The book of endings / Leslie Harrison.
Description: First edition. | Akron, Ohio : University of Akron Press, 2017. |
  Series: Akron series in poetry
Identifiers: LCCN 2016026149 (print) | LCCN 2016033470 (ebook) | ISBN 9781629220628
  (hardback : alk. paper) | ISBN 9781629220635 (paperback : alk. paper) |
  ISBN 9781629220642 (ePDF) | ISBN 9781629220659 (ePub)
Classification: LCC PS3608.A78357 A6 2017 (print) | LCC PS3608.A78357 (ebook) |
  DDC 811/.6—dc23
LC record available at https://lccn.loc.gov/2016026149

∞The paper used in this publication meets the minimum requirements of ANSI/NISO
z39.48–1992 (Permanence of Paper).

Cover: *Raven Feathers* by Mike O'Connell, © 2015. Reproduced with permission. Cover design
by Amy Freels.

The Book of Endings was designed and typeset in Garamond with Cooper Hewitt display by Amy
Freels. It was printed on sixty-pound natural and bound by Bookmasters of Ashland, Ohio.

Contents

Center Panel

Afford yourself what you can carry out.
A coward and a coda share a word.
We get our ugliness from fear.
We get our danger from the lord.
—Heather McHugh

[I keep throwing words at the problem because words]

To list the day full of ravens and crows is to attempt

meaning as if words could mend themselves the way

the window eventually cures itself of frost I don't know

how to make anything how to make anything better

the mourning doves on the lines suspect nothing about

the way machines keep throwing voices how objects

contain how the wires conduct silence and spark

to say vessels contain is to attempt again to make

this storm of trees and sky into prophesy is to advocate

for an undivided world unfold the dead hawk's wing

and ask it about flight ask the killdeer how it came

to equate love with broken love with panic safety

with leading with leading the dangerous on

dear Cassandra the page is funnel pitcher or cloud

into which I keep pouring the trees the listing birds

the way they keep refusing to mean the way I want

to mean anything other than this other than this much

silence the way the page both contains refuses the stain

Left Panel

[December]

That was the year that ice begot ravens singly in pairs and crows

a gathering flock fed well of the damaged trees their desperate fruit

come to trouble what little sleep come to comfort the stoneheavy days

come to this house locked in ice the stacked snow sealed over so cold

the owls died off from the branches such delicate flowers falling and

falling silent no call and no response I think the bones of birds must

trouble this earth more than most those hollow bore needles fallen

eventually white on white snow and still the cold thickens strange slow

tidal sea pierced above by a different falling the Geminids December's

bright detritus going down in snowflake fire as if a wake could be

a lovely thing as if broken were just another glittering season

into which you bundle the children into which you carry them to stare

to see a sky quiet and on fire in this winter of no more miracles

in this season of so much beauty such harm

[God speaks]

I laced the world in water water in ice ice in long slow

nights ancient and faintly aglow I gave you this world

gave you who are also mostly water into this world

candled your souls against the ice and the dark matter

against the fields strewn with artifacts and timothy-

grass fields deep with creatures with star-shaped with

star intoxicated flowers I made the heavens and set

them to rain set the moon like a clock passing often

into shadow I filled the least and the greatest places

with secret creatures let you read in stone my own

book of the dead I gave the serpent a tongue so that

you might learn to speak I wanted you to love

his sad machinations his thousand thousand ribs

like some holy cathedral some architecture of tunnel

gate and teeth I made your bodies gorgeous made you

as arrows and fletched your hearts with his sturdy

circling ribs listen as all my beloved creatures whisper

and call through the sun through snow listen to the wind

coming in listen hard and someone will name the bow

[Summa mathematica]

—The camera is a kind of clock (Barthes)

A house like a photograph isolates contains such a small piece

thin slice of the whole immense place the lens erases with ease

the Alps Thames Taiga your neighbor your neighborhood

how much of even the very local gets excluded by frame

by walls roof and door it is a kind of vanishing an equation

that returns a tiny private remainder a number quite close

to nothing inside the house there is no lake no old groaning oak

no stone or stone marker nor crescent moon of meadow meeting

shore even the approach road is gone each arrival a mystery of

the simple arithmetic of increase in this room in this bed I am

full of babies exactly the way the house returns a nearly null set

which is to say I lost my mother and never became one either

which is to say the stacked albums are small museums they're

happy set pieces remainders returned from that thing we call

the past the cakes cheerfully going up in flames the trees too

festive and on fire the dead still here and all that will come left out

[I would drive to your grave]

I would drive to your grave but your grave is the crash

the froth foam pebbles small rocks the sand smoothed

soothed each rising each leaving tide you lie in the ocean

the water in the waves your home the stern the back

the wake of a boat those curled white lines of leaving

I would visit your grave but your grave is a single blue

afternoon of passing isles the green and granite shores

I would come to your grave but your grave is the fire

oh mother it is cold tonight and I have no heart

for this burning for the fine sift of ash which is all

that comes back all that comes after I would visit

your house but your things are missing are missing

your touch as your eyes failed I brought you lights

and I would see again that brightness I would drive

to your grave but I am your grave your marker

oh mother I am your stone

[Imagine]

My goals today are modest

          attend the sky for signs of failing falling

signs the buildings remain at ease

          comfortable abutments guarding against

               so much endless space

their blank faces intentionally broken open in windows

          such casual such pretty risk

*

The blind   wear sunglasses

             darkness being one thing

exempt from multiplication

         objects in mirrors   are often

    closer than they appear

what follows

    does so in ways both intimate and dangerous

movie stars wear shades

         windows without history

forgetting the arc lamp of the past forgetting

     recognition

         was never a matter for such tiny disguises

*

The sky all day

       the sky keeps showing off   amusing itself

with the usual bag of tricks

          the city stands below   stands

      in shadow   somewhere small switches are thrown

and the stars muscle their way into being

             into being seen   again

our ancient coming attractions   a million years or more

      in the making   and in the dying   in the dying night

we go out into the lighted dark   we go   over the details

     we make extensive notes   excuses   amends

we never needed

      to imagine the past

   but still we do

[There are things you love]

There are things you love but they are rarely if ever

the right things your favorite color that mottled dapple

that fleeting purpleyellowblackgreen that exists only inside

skin in the wake of harm the bittern's upstretched neck

a gesture you can't get over its offer of concealment that

also references danger for years you've loved the goose

found at pond edge found at clouded blueblack daybreak

its neck curved back head tucked as if risk as if the dark

were nowhere were nothing to fear but then you saw

feathers like petals like fasteners fallen open fallen

to curl and drift in those shallows whatever befell had

nothing of violence in it rather a quiet fading a still slip

down or away rocked by ripple by wind feathers and flesh

coming undone unmended coming into water such a small

such a slight armada the body given over sanctified

at almost dawn coming finally almost whole almost safe

almost to daybreak and to shore

[Pray]

I test the reality of this slippery day

                              already easing out of reach

I pick minutes for hours

                    in the meadow and this does not

                                    help me

the clouds the trees   the trees rasp

                        like ancient crickets

phlegmy in the way that old things

                      are never really loud

look at the horses

               look

                  at their four fragile knees

kneel later

            kneel

            kneel when they've given you a box

a closet built of dirt   its weighty

                      stone   handle

then you can kneel then you can pray

pray for the rest of your life

kneeling

for years

as the meadow appears

and falls under snow   pray with a voice

full of dried leaves full   of falling water

voice of new

growth new snow

pray

pray as hard as you can   to the horses

skittering

startled

away

[Take eat]

Take eat he said for this is my body and we thought

he meant us we who are also drawn to the table

always craving olive mango bread rare flesh and wine

but it is the earth replies by making way by taking in

by each endless indifferent yes shaped like one more

rectilinear hole as if the digging alone could constitute

a form of prayer or arcane mathematics a series of

n-dimensional spaces the volume infinite the collapse

therefore also always ending in infinity ending as a

zero sum game a dimension into which every thing

you ever loved is poured like wine blood like some

kind of sacrament microbes turn fruit potent turn flesh

to sludge then seed in physics momentum and position

define degrees of freedom delete momentum and what

remains is one person in a box is a system collapse

is sky holding ground holding stone holding hole

holding hands holding on black hole without end

the earth gave us everything took it back again

[The orphan child eats blueberries in Vermont]

Jeffrey's Ledge is full of rising full of convection conversion full

of peculiar geologic detail full of sudden shallows those undersea

hills a vertical face against which the ocean comes in force in tide

in wind a long slow grind toward shore full in summer of whales

come for the krill the fish come with new beings their young

in tow and taking milk what falls in water is never water is ash

is death is flesh sent through the fire to fall a year later like rain

on each slow leviathan is grain by minute grain sunk or gathered

to be carried was this what you wanted most mother wanted of

and for all that remains did you want the long slow travel mournful

song a vast time-lapse failure an extinction colder and more alone

than anything ought to be did you want finally to be carried off

by something other something greater than this dis-ease of failing

heart of lungs filling again did you want ease peace a home a place

in this the swallowing element no breath no longer any need did

you want finally to be cradled by something benevolent something

large taken with such strange such falling grace away the body

mimics the heart stutters says sad sad so sad the body swan dives

trips the body falls into such far mornings as this your death already a year old the tide at slack grief the mist clinging to the fields

the circling hills the body sits with strangers eats blueberries

bluer than your ocean blue as the vacancy sign you never meant

to hang in all our lives the blue of the sky picked up and held

by the water this predawn leak of light so like the tint of your lips

the color of oxygen-lack the final absence of air cyanosis they call it

the heart submerged and drowning the ship of your life going down

cyanosis for this rising storm cyanosis like cyan the printer's least

stable ink cyan from *kyanous* which is Greek which just means blue

[To say]

There are dead creatures all over and under this earth

to say your heart is broken is to translocate sorrow

to honor the stutter you carry always in its own cage

beast of the gaps unrested hesitations to say your heart

is broken is to say the river never wanted those particular

dead and is to also say the field full of mice going in fear

of all that has wings is also full of stubble the grain taken

dead and leavened by hands by time to say your heart

is broken is to see inside your mind all that is gone all

that has become the shadow of wings all that will never

again appear to say your heart is broken is to wish to end

the uneven engine mend it into silence or steady purr

is to say something about the difficulty of repair is to say

your heart your memories the field the river the bodies

are all intact and can never be saved no matter what

[Practice]

They keep throwing their bodies at all the versions of water

river lake bath puddle ocean even every snowy hill the children

remember water the children remember and cry carry me

with pursed bird mouths with sharp bird voices with faces

tuned to the looming tide the children practice being creatures

being creatures again the children have already been taught

already know how to fold their bones into clothes lean their

knees into pews their hearts over desks fold hands into attitudes

like prayer cursive or like a fist released into sleep the children

curl fetal again soft again cradled by the hammock moon

the knit mesh of stars nights they write field guides to lairs

and all the secrets creatures keep

[Ötzi]

When the hay wain wound its way across the hill

you failed to follow because winter meant

fallow meant cold frozen fields meant then lost

in the icy heights meant also found means found

five thousand three hundred years after they knapped

the blade and you made room for it in your body

winter means preservation means the soul

on ice means dead is only one definition means

geography is only one explanation

the seasons turn the season turns colder

the mirrors fog over when I breathe meaning

I can be visible be present but

not while yet I live and true north is nothing

but a lodestone just another sharp implement

pointing to lost those nearly endless years

the body retrieved from the ice rope marks

and scars still visible in the flesh

and pollen that necessary sturdy fruit

says head down in a glacier one blade

in your hand and one in place of your heart

says when first you were lost the blackthorn

was in flower as was the larch

[Coda]

And it came to pass after this that the chariots broke the hours

into horses broke them to the rein bit the hackamore the whip

it was already and still is as if nothing had ever happened and

the chariots were made of gold of air of geese barking across

the speckled sky the crows look up order in their dictionary

of branch and cloud and answers keep not happening for any

of us beside the river they closed the road so now we walk

and the river moves and moves on and does not and the cool

drumskin sky turns gray then grayer still and then the thunder

comes

[Wilt thou play with him as with a bird]

For I have loved the blade with all my crippled

with all my awkward soul loved it for the shine

sheen for the ease and grace of doing what it was

made to do for I have loved the stubborn womb

its beloved intent have loved the hope and then

learned to love the lack for I have loved the water

the way it comes to me comes for me in all its

liquid mystery for I have loved what the water

loves its myriad vessels sky basin runnel channel

and vein for all it claims and contains for I have

loved its muscular flex its rise coil and fall so like

Leviathan's mighty desperate heart for I have loved

Leviathan for being only for being exactly

what god hated and what he made for being

water's own knife this wild unholy blade

Right Panel

[When trees are dead they are]

When trees are dead they are wood straight-grained

solid flesh when we die we are of what use what matter

no shelter is built of our bones of our going such small pieces

taken instead into soil lair into ground wind sand salt or sea

the world barely remade in our unfastening these bodies

so ill-suited to use better suited to waste to want to hunger

the way our minds attach themselves with claw and teeth

to such thin things as hope to having met one man once again

and once again to having invented desire that terrible bludgeon

that blade so rare to desire the essential simple things

rice for the table blanket for the bed we want hands instead

we want whatever we meant by love the bodies' tectonic

collision friction the frisson of touch subsumed subducted

in the plates the wine the meal we are all so practiced

at falling at coming slowly coming both apart and undone

skin by limb by falling we gather trees plant them deep

for love oh love marry me instead to the forest marry

me please to the fencepost the mast the table or the rack

[Carnation lily lily rose]

The trees drop wilting petals this confetti pink and red

lilac and rose as pollen too drifts and falls turns every

puddle urinous the drunken bees swerve through

the ruined afternoon and you keep asking me to believe

keep calling me an optimist but how can I count on this

count each happy family by their shuttered windows their

thoroughly locked doors how can I count smoke as evidence

of warmth of fire count on the way desire drunk on pollen

drunk on the season staggers and stings count on the way

strangers keep wanting to touch my hair make a wish you say

make a wish but the planets careen on through constellations

disrupting the given stories then changing them back again

black holes open and close like the beaks of baby birds

ravenous and crashing from their nests their naked skin

the cold pink of furled petals how is it that the world keeps

coming to this these long spring afternoons how can I count

them as evidence of anything oh love you think I wanted this

I never wanted this I didn't know how to want any of this

[Sisyphus in love]

At first it was the stone the rough stubble skin of it the call

and response the stone's going its perpetual coming back

the insistence of the fact of it shaping each piece of his body

muscle bone rough hands their slow curve toward its weight

the way it wanted the way it wanted him never farther away

than the length of his arm the cheek to cheek dance the way

he wore its dust and scent breathed it in and then it was the hill

the way he cut his name his story over time the furze worn

in tracks how it defined his being a tipped horizon the sky

obscured the way it wore each cloud the world's difficult

weather as jewel and costume the myriad ways it refused

to move be moved seduced or yield he loved it most for that

and then it was the song those lovely small waves that flutter

felt against the ear his skin that it could also sometimes be

like this those pulsing waves such fine such slight adjustments

it took his breath tuned turned his ear to hear and overhear

those notes upon his shore his skin and then it was the stone again

[Eve]

If the angels came there would be no kindness they are

after all also without mercy pity they are warriors soldiers

of wing beak and sword they are griffins of the lord endlessly

taking sides come unto all of this world to do his bidding

he has no interest in rescue how obvious that has become he has

no interest in the seed its vanishing its chance random choice

of fate either ground cradled or ground down in the bird's

churning belly seed is food is blood is muscle is waiting

to become flesh its own or someone else's seed is always

fuel in the metabolic fire the apple a womb encounters

her teeth she taught herself to eat god taught her to bleed

[Stutter]

I said love because it came closest said leave

because you did we do this peeling off each

from each each from suddenly other said

come back but meant don't go I said dead

and meant every one of those instances of

vanishment how the dead swim away from us

in time their tide their closed wooden boats

I said tide but tide was never right said tide

because we have no word for that kind of

unforgiving away I said tether when I meant

anchor when I meant stay but when I said stay

one thing I meant was against confusion

against yet another loss I meant two-faced

Janus January's god of fallen gates of trying

to look both ways and when I said farewell

I meant again don't go but it was too late I was

here in the hall this tunnel full of mirrors glass

and strange made-up faces and when I thought

funhouse I meant its opposite I meant this

rusty carnival town the men so sad they paint

their smiles in place they paint their faces

white paint their eyes wide and full of crying

[Sirens]

I'm not Penelope married to faith married to waiting

bound in fine soft strands of silk dyed and stretched

in my world longing has teeth and fins has a taste

for blood longing is a room built entirely of knives

all edges facing in all points afire and also somehow

held to the vessel in my world sirens are the town criers

saying something's happened and maybe to you saying

someone got too close to danger sirens are the past tense

of rescue meaning clean-up in aisle three where

the glass racks have fallen before the mast where the sea

rose up between the meat and the waiting where the bed

refused as usual to become the boat where the dead

drape and tangle in the rigging the sheets in the loom

and the sirens gather to wail flicker and shine where they

gather together to sing of damage to sing us home

[Parable]

God the child threw fits threw storms like broken toys

around his room god the child rested slept as in that old joke

like a baby waking often to cry for who or what made and fed

bathed and kept him god the child was already older than any

thing he caused to be made he left his crib his prison of flesh

for other states god the child made and loves the master who

to save the nation clips the wings of ravens chains them into

the certainties of space and stone no more wingéd oars chewing

the sky the creak of flight made quiet made deafening by

its absence the way the stars make the dark into synaesthetic

noise god the child gathers the clipped feathers broken wings

sews them into cloak blanket story god the child kills

the ravenmaster in the fullness in the boredom of his days

and the black beaks open and silence is stolen into rasping

speech and this this is where love is born where love comes from

as the birds are chained to the tower so we are chained

to each other and god the child makes another ravenmaster

to love and maim the birds and god grows older grows

tired rests his sick head on piles and soft piles of broken

wings hoarse voices of our clipped and necessary feathers

[Charm for a spring storm]

I am tamping down the earth I am patting it back

with the flat side of a blade I am burying you

with all the other dead because hydrangeas because

lilacs and tiny cinquefoil stars and when you call

and when you say you want to meet and I say yes

but suddenly the snow prevents your arrival I simply

dig another hole though the ground is unwilling though

the ground is cold and indifferent and when you called

I was busy I was combing my hair there in the garden

I was inventorying the bones saying *sacrum* saying

iliac crest saying *sternal notch* I was watching I was waiting

for the moon for the moon to turn my hair even more

silver I never thought I'd get this old and now

nothing I own has ever smelled of you I was

in the garden and it was snowing and the whole world

was on fire it was spring and I was adding stones to

my pockets trying to teach the ground trying to teach

the water that this is how you love you don't give up

you don't give back you take the bones hold them tight

you cut a way in weigh the body down weigh down

the body with a body you fold the garden in around you

like a blanket like a prayer you come over here you stay

[Landscape with falling birds]

All the voices in the world humming in the radio waves in the wires

tangle braid and knot and not one is you trying to find me every one

is the dropped call lost before it sets tongue to bell pulse to pulse

they sing the voices in the wires in the waves in the sky I hear them

singing all the time operatic and frantic and I cannot sleep for all

the singing when I wake from not sleeping a hundred thousand birds

have fallen dead from the wires their branches if someone could gather

the dead the rain of feathers and flight would drown us all and

there would be no boat then the boat would come too late the captain

demanding a payment that payment would be stop trying to forget

remember all the time for ever the sound of his voice remember

as if it were the last light before you were blind and I would say

but wait what is a voice what is light they are uninhabitable

you cannot live there and he would say yes and he would say

remember as if it were the only perfect light so what I see is not

candle star sun incandescent neon acetylene moon no buzz hum

flicker heat is instead the scent of all that died mixed with time

and pressure poured into glass and fragile poured against a wick and lit

[That]

That this is the morning in which nothing much

that the sky is still there and the water dresses

accordingly that only at night does the water rest

vanish from sight that the stars are too small too far

to register there that all our names too are writ

invisibly on water that abiding requires more hope

than I can possibly acquire that hope is not a thing

with feathers that hope is a thing with a fist a thin

crust sketched over oceans that hope is what despair

uses for bait come in hope says the water's fine

that hope is the blood with which you write letters

that start dear sea dear ocean stop asking so fucking

much that hope is a telegram delivered by men

in pairs men in uniform a telegram that says missing

stop that says once again presumed lost stop

[Venice]

It is spring will be soon and Venice is sinking

into its own ocean the past the places I may

never go I am terrified he is ill is dying he jokes

about mortality every time we speak and the Venice

that dreams watery cool and pastel inside my head

sinks each time a little further into the flooding chambers

of that carefully constructed organ the dumb pump

that sends both of us out on our separate trajectories

separate for so long now the pump I blame for all the ways

it will has and did fail behind my own mortal breasts

I feel the water the river the world taking greedy and rising

and if born to drown what could this small lump matter

what could his skittering away from futures just as I as a child

couldn't bear to see the shining things on offer for others

who could pay matter and now when I would pay

almost any price now here this moment everything comes

back to the pump in waves in which both of us and Venice

will have fallen but please God not yet below the surface

another ruined thing necessary and more beautiful

[The horses]

I wanted to ask how do I do this how do I keep doing this

how do I stop I once required the moon no once your voice

moved the moon for hours across the skylight and the stove

burned itself out and the stars followed suit eight hours passed

and the moon passed the glass filled instead with clouded day

and both of us so tired still not saying goodbye and my ear

days later still red and tender the hot phone I held going down

again into the cooling house the house the baby squirrels came

all that spring into for warmth caught and taken in a box kept

for nothing but that to the barn and set down in the hay

and fallen feed the horses retired to other homes the barn

where tack hung in the shapes of backs necks mouths and brows

as though the horses had not gone but become instead invisible

I had never been happier disliked the intervals of silence and sun

I no longer own a barn a skylight full of the moon a house

that squirrels seek out we both still own the means but

what keeps happening is the moon the day and the moon again

and it wasn't the horses turning into ghosts it wasn't

[Touch me now]

One day I wake

       I walk   forward   carrying

a narrative carrying an end

           a hole   ten years deep

     and sleep has made for it   a lid

fragile thin plastic wrap   a skin graft   a patch

        inside

the hole is dark and full of stars

           is dark and full

 of scars this body

       grows a garden of badly barely healed

feelings

     I mean skin I mean

          go ahead touch me now

for I am wild

[Was it ice]

The season settles in strips the trees of leaves the heart

of the matter is weather I have been wind sheared storm

wracked thrown off course and down I have been all

river no shore what drowns you is not the water but

the ice this strict difficult surface refusing to let you go

let you grow replacement parts for what's been cut away

glaciers planted boulders huge stones that bubble up

from the soil I mean the soul from which you make

the walls high and thick from which you fill the holes

till the soil for some semblance of hope your role

in all of this is dimly understood the ways that safety

arises or has passed you by you are neither glacier

nor ground nor harbor breakwater shelter siren

or cave is it comfort or touch that you crave

was it ice that held you down or was it love

[Once]

Once I caught fireflies in a summer meadow thunderheads building

the night harrowing the sky once in a different night I played at hiding

was sought by the wrong boy once summer's thin fabric and hands

taught me loathing of my own flesh once I was caught and bound

by a stranger once I bound myself to a man I only thought I loved

in the haze and fog of insects and dying stars once all my choices

were proven wrong in the crinkling grass in the shining moss

up high once a mountain taught me my bones and breath

taught me to breathe once I learned from a mountain how to leave

[Parable]

Sometimes when I wake crawl from the beloved dark everyone else

has gone out as if winter were never danger as if ice were of no

consequence everyone has gone out as in candle as in light fire

door as if in need of more contact with the ground everyone has

knelt frozen in the snow just so many statues vivid in treeshadow

each body vacant each body a cold patience and what happens next

is that I too go out among them I count each one where they kneel

I walk forbidden somehow to touch shoulder touch cheek wipe snow

from where it drifts against open eyes I count by outlining shadows

trace each thin penumbra into the snow move on to the next move on

late into grayblue dusk as the cold gathers as the wind moves in

as overhead these old desert leaves rattle where they cling mutter

this bitter rosary of life before it came down to just this useless

holding on when the moon comes when the moon brightens but

does not warm I stop to rest I stop to sleep I curl sheltered from

the wind on this the quiet side of one stranger or another

[Epiphany]

This day   night

             this place

is a world

        of still air

              of smoke   like ghosts

gathered

       over houses

            a place in which you

      are like the smoke

              which is to say

                  mostly gone

which is to say   the bitter end

              of a terrible fire

        call

            for wind   pray for it

lay me down

       right here

            in the holy night   under

those clear old skies

        lay me down

in the town square   let

   the smoke

     grow thin as an old pall

pall as in cover

    over chalice or coffin

       pall meaning

wear out wear thin   as smoke

     as smoke   caught

in the risen

   in this finally risen   in this   the wind

Center Panel

[Actias luna]

Dear god dear ghost dear ghostgod and dearly departed

dear mother and dear water you own each other now

tangled in blue molecular hollows in the always arriving

rain we own your porches your wornwood docks all those

swaybacked summer places dear god you are not were not

the water not coming always toward us in blood and tide

in particles and waves dear god you should know

I'm no one's shore no one's ocean dear darkness dear forest

dear pale flutter dear light-impaled luna dear all the secret

ways of wood and water dear fire and dear myriad scars

dear god this is not faith this is a moth born silent born

without mouth this is a soul in painful molt to winged hungry

and dying in the dark this is a single green angel lost in chemic

quest in the narrow June night this is the white bright cross

stained with a thousand tiny lives tiny deaths this is the light

we mistake for light this is the might as well be dead beloved

dear god dear thief you stole them both dear god dear wrecker

no matter what you think what you might have thought

this is not a love letter

[Parable]

I wake and once again the trees have come the trees

have once again grown through me a tiny forest tiny

tangled copse come to populate all the windswept

all the empty spaces dendritic roots curl around cells

as if around stones and the furling tender leaves

with their hungry wait for light and now the trees

fill with birds whose wings I feel as faint capillary

flutter whose songs rustle in the blood autumn now

and the leaves loosen begin their fall the tiny spiders

move in set about their careful work stitching leaves

back to branches mending the quilted sky the geese

travel over and in the woods the mist descends

everything is indistinct all bleached and pale the mist

tastes in the muscles in the throat like a chill when

the mist dissipates it takes everything with it branches

leaves spiders their sticky useless sutures even the trees

are gone the spaces full of snow and now the snow too

is gone the spaces are meadows again are empty again

and now this is who this is what this is all I am

[Over]

When he's done with them the angels shred in the wind the angels die

like rifles crack sharp and hard metal brittle in bitter cold the angels

die on the wheel the cross the rack when it's over his cold puppets

hang in their mute strings their snarled their tattered wings their teeth

gnaw briefly at the gate they wail and beg but nothing comes back

the angels learn then how to pray the angels learn why prayer requires

flesh blood and bone requires bone cut out carved and offered up

pray they say pray as if you meant it as if the bone each prayer

is etched upon were not your own but the arm shin or rib of some

sad and lovely child some fragile perfect being go ahead they say

call the baby in from the abbey walk the colt in from his life between

the meadow and the sky walk him away from the places he believes

he is both safe and at home hide the blade behind your crumbling

your serpent spine and pray pray as if his faith his love his grace

his reckless racing life depends upon it and know that it does and

that it does not matter

[This I know]

That the horses   that   somehow

            fear begets grace   is born

               is even now   running

*

that the dead

      that there is   nothing left

       that the dead tether   only each other

          anchor   only oceans   only stones

*

that even beloved   that beloved

           lasts   lasts as long as

          not very

*

      that you choose   to go on

          or do not

*

that the blade   can cut   but

      the blade

          severs nothing   that scars

   are reins roads   are maps

*

that scar is halter   scar is tether   is   weathered weal

                white rope   that scar

        is never really   going to heal

[What I mean]

You must understand when I say heart say broken say

angel god when I say love and say death those huge

small words you should distrust something language

me the ravine vast gap between what flickers in the mind

and what stumbles into language stumbles the way

I stumble into the woods walk lost walk directionless

walk allowed each day only to listen and come later

aching crazed and at peace to some edge some river

of water dirt or rarely pavement and nobody asks and

still what tolls through the night is what did you do today

and you remake your day into story into language I walked

I say I sent the blood to punish the heart that fine red engine

I sent the body against again the world that huge construct

one fraction of which is all I will ever travel I sent the body

so I could feel it there in the forest thickets glades and rivers

feel the heat the heart's whole house shaken whole house

shuddering I say god say angel though they may not exist

as such though nothing is speaking to speaking for or

through me so what name should I make for what got caught

in this bleak this grief if not heart which is whole which is never yet broken never even empty listen dear when I say heart

what I mean is maybe boat that thin-sailed machine tumbled

in a storm's grinding path when I say broken what I mean

is small craft warning is storm beyond any storm this body

can make or endure what I mean is too far from shore is maybe

no shore no ocean is sounding again those old familiar depths

and when I say depth what I mean is fathom meaning a measure

of how far down to dig a grave meaning the span of a man's arms

meaning stranded go deeper meaning I don't understand

[Because in all your life you've lived]

Because in all your life you've lived always the same twelve hours

though you remember them otherwise the years with their numbers

the months the anonymous weeks because you don't understand how

so many differences accrete in the sameness of days because the barn

is again empty the meadow strewn with both sweet and rue because

the horses acquiesce daily to those thin fences because holy means

wholly most surely alone because you believe the horses to be small

gods and because the gods this morning have rolled in mud and have

thundered but again did not jump because when you speak of the horses

the angels bare and gnash their sharpened teeth because the dark belongs

only to itself but the stars don't mind if you call them your own because

you are the water living between the ice and so many stony places

because you too are all tide and fence all rise and rail because we assemble

the world with imperfect senses because therefore we can never fully

understand because there is a fence between one moment and the next

and this is the fence we acquiesce to and we name that fence time the way

we say event horizon for all that which cannot escape because the horses

did once escape and swam from the sea in storm and wreck and because

they never again left but once oh once were never had never been here

[Snowfields]

And I wonder sprawled on the curved recurved back

of the hill the towers of clouded sky crushing the horizon

flat I want to know how to strip the griefstorm from the flesh

flense the spirit scrape it down to the clean bone unbreaking

make it take in stride another raw dawn these days of snow

on cold on frozen take in stride this place of glass and ice

this place knit stitched pierced by the shadows of all those

departed birds begin again to assemble linens pillows

blankets scarves the small soft comforts cushions cradles

learn how to lay me down in something other than danger

other than fury ice and risk learn to stop dropping this body

into snowfields making these empty shapes learn to stop

waiting for them to be filled

[Let the blue earth spin]

The heart beats its   thin fists

        against the bones   the rails

     the heart   the heart rails   against this

  silence   this   absence   I count

        every   imaginable

thing

    stars scars streetlights   the endless   succession

    of nights   the heart we say

    the heart   for what

     gets chipped   by the facts of the

matter

you let the blue earth   spin   you let   time zone you

   let this clotted   afternoon

  unspool

   because what if   the soul's deciduous

what if antlers   leaves and teeth

   what if   something

  decorates that way   breathes through this

  what if this   is the way you fall   what if

he lives   on   what if   they all do   what if

                    this incantation of starlings

                                                            decanted

into   an   abiding sky

[Things the realtor will not tell the new owner]

When she left she left so many ghosts the whole place is

poisoned with them their stray sadnesses untraceable scents

those cold holes in the very air so when you wake your throat

choked with tears having dreamt some strange some other

beloved you never knew and know is gone and this morning

desperately miss don't panic please please rise instead into

the groundmist walk out among her patient anchored trees

her ghostbear is there but will offer no harm will pace hungry

wary and finally away there too the ghost coyotes who filled

her nights with difficult with strange music you'll hear her

ghostbirds the hawk as a tiny falling wind the owls of winter

dying like prayers the morning flight of songbirds who carve

her shape into the yard with their swerving whose young

are born into the feel and smell of her hair rise and walk

through all of it to the lake next door you'll find her spot

on shore you'll let those borrowed those inherited tears

join hers the ones she shed so long ago you'll let small fish

rise to the drops salted and falling it will all feel familiar

to them and like she's come home so go about your days

in phantom pain as if your own life had been badly amputated then badly sewn back but when you weary of it slip

into that room ease down on the bed the one she left

and left and left again when you lie down you choose the other

side you sleep in sleep your arm reaches to where her back

once curved you pull her impossibly toward you nest rest

like that but wherever it is she is she and all her creatures

sleep on uncomforted and alone

[Salt]

Encased in snow flakes breaking from cloud sky

falling still a practiced collapsing too cold to cling

fine and weightless waking again from dreams of you

cheeks and the slight hollows at the edge of sight

stained salt stained like the ground stained white

once the world thought snow and snow was all

it wanted humans salt the roads to make them safe

for travel an exit strategy part cold part slow bitter

ribbon white for journeying white for grief Carthage

sacked and salted and the Portuguese duke of Aviero's

house pulled down his gardens sown with salt a stone

for betrayal saying here on this land nothing may be built

for all time I don't want to spend the days in the fields

trying to plant the nights seeding the ground with salt

if memory is what I have I'd rather do without

[Dear god I ask]

nothing for myself as much of what I love is changed

to salt and stone and ocean only the meadows the deer

the flicker of trees in timelapse light flicker of trains

these endless metal departures dear lord I ask only this

for myself that the stars come evenings out of the black

dark sky the snow fall enough to muffle the ping of pipes

freezing in the walls that the barn dear lord I ask that

there always be a barn built of the carved up bones

the sky once leaned so heavily upon the wood weathered

into silver into slivers and whorls be indifferent to us

dear lord be gentle with your angels for they know

only how to fail sing lullabies to the broken the sleep

deprived the flailing failing the falling and the galloping

along sing lullabies to the storm climbing each horizon

neither bridle nor ever try to tame our beloved Leviathan

nor any one of your strange creatures let us run if that be

our desire let us run into grass and gale and sharp wire

fences into long crumbling afternoons let us run

back into what we thought was home even when

even though sometimes as now the barn be made

wholly be made entirely of fire

[Bezoar]

Tell me how to want this world this world that swallows

so much that sends so much of what I love into the ground

tell me how to want the rain again how to hope when

the rain has never fallen not once for 180 days tell me

how to want that ocean of days tell me how to love the graves

the ones we collect into grassy matched sets in dry green seas

and the others the ones we disperse into trees and creatures

as if ash were delicious as if when he said take eat he meant

burn this flesh to cinder for this is my body for this is

the future forget the blood the flesh the wind the wine

swallow instead every ground-down bone make of love make

of despair a bezoar make of the body a body make of a hole

a potion against the poison of all the days just now dawning

all the days of coming dust of hunger of nothing left to hunger for

[Wrong]

How the ground gives some things back cicadas for instance

how seventeen years of gone years of nowhere here years

of not cicada and now the swarm now frailglass wings and

now mouth and now devour the flowers too tucked sucked

back down coffined in their own pockets their purses of

save and wait wait all summer fall all winter and then again

they come somehow different somehow exactly the same

how worms curl nest and feast in fallen whalebone how not

one of them becomes the whale lost in the pressured dark

how the mouth of the river dies in the mouth of the ocean

this sad equation of water unequal to water how the swan's

obscene neck curls in the muck like a question the world

keeps refusing to answer or always answers wrong

[Invocation]

And sometimes the soul quiets in the cells curls furls

idle silent and still sometimes the soul comes to rest

and what wakes after another night of darksinging skies

is star-nosed mole is maybe dormouse sparrow or wren

some creature of nearly no color nearly no consequence

a being entirely simply itself a being no longer in love

with its own event horizons the soul wakes tangled

in roads dirty with oceans and season under a sky

wan and pale the small furry soul pokes its head

into the cold is reborn sans teeth eats gravel small stones

for the quiet grinding deep inside oh small spidersilk soul

soul of the feathered frost and the good brown garden

sticky persistent soul small hollow-boned ghost of sky

and journey oh slight soul teach me how to hold on

to all of this teach me please oh lord how to let go

[Nest]

And I want to say that the heart hangs there at the end of things

wavering a little a bit unsteady this vessel this hotel for transients

this lodge that takes the shape of a wasp's nest paper and swaying

and I want to say hey listen to this my body is a tree full of branchings

full of venom hum and sting full of wild creatures hunger leaves

and leavings hey listen I say hold that soft nautilus ear just so and

you can hear this colony collapse all the tiny dyings can hear

this lantern hung hissing and unlit when a light deserts its wick

the heart goes dark the heart becomes just one more vessel waiting

to sail waiting for the wind listen to the word vessel its desire

its desire to carry various cargoes its need to practice departures

hush now the sails are going up the sun is going down the people

on shore wave small scraps of fabric they're white in the dusk

like wings they're white in the dark like surrender

∾

Notes

The quatrain that opens the book is from Heather McHugh's poem "Etymological Dirge," published in *The Father of the Predicaments* (Middletown, Conn.: Wesleyan University Press, 1999), 77.

The phrase *Take, eat* appears several places in the Bible (Matthew 26:26, I Corinthians 11:24, and Mark 14:22). They are Jesus' words, spoken to his disciples at the Last Supper.

Ötzi is the name given to a well-preserved, ancient body found in a glacier in the Alps between Austria and Italy in 1991. He is Europe's oldest human mummy.

The title of *[Wilt thou play with him as with a bird]* is from Job 41:5.

Carnation, Lily, Lily, Rose is the name of a painting by John Singer Sargent.

[Sirens] owes a debt to a draft of a poem by Sasha West.

[That] references a poem by Emily Dickinson, and also refers to what is inscribed on the gravestone of John Keats.

[Touch me now] references a line from the movie *2001: A Space Odyssey.*

[Actias luna] references a memorial cross on the grounds of Sewanee: The University of the South. *Actias luna* is the Latin name for the luna moth.

Acknowledgments

I am grateful to the editors of the following journals, where some of these poems first appeared, sometimes in different forms.

Antioch Review: [I keep throwing words at the problem because words]
Barn Owl Review: [Once], [Venice]
The Bennington Review: [I would drive to your grave]
Birmingham Review: [Landscape with falling birds], [Salt]
Cherry Tree: [Practice], [That]
Connotation Press (A Poetry Congeries): [Otzi], [Over], [What I mean]
The Delmarva Review: [Parable], [Summa mathematica], [Wilt thou play with him as with a bird]
FIELD: [December]
Gulf Coast: [Was it ice]
The Kenyon Review: [There are things you love]
Kenyon Review Online: [Eve]
Narrative: [Charm for a spring storm]
The New Republic: [Stutter], [Things the realtor should not tell the new owner]
Pleiades: [Actias luna]
Plume: [To say]
Orion: [Parable]
Subtropics: [God speaks]
Water~Stone Review: [Imagine], [Wrong]
West Branch: [Because in all your life you've lived], [Bezoar], [Coda], [Sisyphus in love], [Take eat]
West Branch Wired: [Invocation], [The orphan child eats blueberries in Vermont]
Zocalo Public Square: [The horses], [Nest]

[Dear god I ask] was first published in the anthology *Before the Door of God*, edited by Jay Hopler and Kimberly Johnson (New Haven, Conn.: Yale University Press, 2015), 381.

[Salt] is a limited edition broadside created by the Center for Book Arts in New York.

[That] was reprinted on Verse Daily.

[There are things you love] was reprinted on Poetry Daily.

To Mary Biddinger, Jon Miller, Amy Freels, and everyone at The University of Akron Press: My gratitude knows no bounds. Thank you for the care you have taken with my book.

Thanks to Mike O'Connell for the use of his gorgeous photograph.

My profound gratitude to the National Endowment for the Arts; Bucknell University, especially the faculty, staff, and fellows of the Stadler Poetry Center; The Massachusetts Cultural Council; The Maryland State Arts Council; the Bread Loaf Writers' Conference; the Sewanee Writers' Conference; and the National Parks Service, especially Margaret Eissler and all the rangers, who shared their beloved Yosemite with me. These are gifts whose magnitude far exceeds their declared valued. This book would not exist without all of you.

It would also not exist without the faith and friendship of the beloved tribe, especially David Bergman, Jennifer Clarvoe, Michael Downs, Jehanne Dubrow, Michelle Gillette, Andrew Hudgins and Erin McGraw, Marsha Lucas, Amelia Ostroff, Diana Park, Hallie Richmond, Will Schutt and Tania Biancalani, Mark Strand, Lisa Sutton, Matt Thorburn, Katrina Vandenberg, Sasha West, Greg Williamson, and Peter Wool. And thanks to C—for the answers to all the questions.

Leslie Harrison holds graduate degrees from the Johns Hopkins University and the University of California, Irvine. Her first book, *Displacement*, won the Bakeless Prize and was published by Mariner Books. A long-time resident of Sandisfield, Massachusetts, she now live and teaches in Baltimore.